Do-It-Yourself User Guide for iPhone 11 and iPhone Pro: Getting the Best of Your Device

By

The Techie Click

Table of Contents

CHAPTER 1: INTRODUCTION

For many years now, Apple Inc. has continuously released one iPhone after the other, while maintaining a chronological numbering for them. Before this most recent release, the previous had been the iPhone 10 and its variants. The iPhone 9 had equally been released earlier and had had its time. Now, Apple has gone on to release the iPhone 11 as its most recent release.

As it always happens, these new upgrades come with several new easy to spot features and yet some not so easily identifiable ones. And as it is with Apple, a new release will always have its variants. This time, the iPhone 11 has both the standard version, the Pro version, and the Pro Max version. However, we shall be putting our focus on the 11 and 11 Pro in this book.

Unlike in the past years where one variant was out, and it took a few months before the other options were brought out, this year's release mode was different. All three variants of the iPhone 11 hit the market at once with their various price ranges. And to be frank, these prices are not very pocket-friendly for a majority of the low and middle-class users.

Unboxing Your New Gadget

The iPhone 11 and its variants come in compact boxes designed to allow for easy differentiation. While the iPhone 11 heralds a white box color design, the 11 Pro and Pro Max boxes sport a matte black color. However, on top of each box is a picture sample of the color you have chosen. So if you bought a red iPhone 11, your box would sport the red replica of your phone at the top.

On opening your box for the first time, you are greeted with your iPhone, whichever variant you choose. The front of your new gadget should have a plastic protective film over it, which was included to militate against scratches. Also included in the box is a white packet that contains two white apple stickers and an operating manual.

In addition to that, you should equally see your Lightning earphones in the usual small boxes. The charger for your new iPhone 11 is also included. For the charging brick, it's an 18 watt USB type C brick while the charging cable is a USB type-c to lightning cable. The 11 Pro version, however, comes with a smaller 5 watts USB lightning charge brick and cable.

Overview of iPhone 11

The iPhone 11, which is more like the standard version of this year's iPhone release, starts at $699 for the 64GB variant of the phone. For the iPhone 11, Apple settled for six colors that it would rock. These colors include Green, Black, Yellow, Red, White, and Purple. It also features an aluminum and glass body design

Starting at $699, the iPhone 11 sheds off $50 from the price of the iPhone XR, which makes it cheaper. In terms of the screen display size, our iPhone 11 comes fitted with a 6.1-inch Liquid Retina HD display with a 1792 x 828 resolution. Its LCD panel is the same as the one the iPhone XR featured last year.

In terms of camera, the iPhone 11 rocks a dual rear camera. While the first is a 12-megapixel wide-angle lens, the other is a 12-MP ultra-wide lens. On the issue of battery capacity, the iPhone 11 rocks a 3,046 mAh battery capacity, which is quite more prominent than that of the XR, which has a capacity of 2,942 mAh.

It supports dual SIM – the first being a Nano-SIM and the other, an e-SIM. It has different variants according to storage capacity, and pricing differs for each – 64GB, 128GB, and 256GB. The iPhone 11 is also built to be dust and water-resistant. We shall look at other features of this gadget in the course of the book.

Overview of iPhone 11 Pro

After the iPhone 11, ranks the iPhone 11 Pro both in terms of price and additional functionalities. Starting at a whopping $999 for its 64GB, just one dollar shy of $1000, the Pro version of the iPhone 11 comes in four distinct colors. These include Silver, Midnight Green, Gold, and Space Gray.

Starting at $999, the iPhone 11 Pro has a 5.8-inch Super Retina XDR screen display size with a 2436 x 1125 resolution. Its price means that it is costlier than the iPhone 11 by as much as $300, and this price is just for the 64GB version of the smartphone. Apple employs the use of stainless steel for the frame of this Pro version while the glass shows off a matte finish.

While the iPhone 11 comes fitted with dual cameras, Apple went a notch forward by adding a third camera to the iPhone 11 Pro. The cameras on the iPhone 11 Pro are 12-megapixel ultra-wide-angle, wide-angle, and telephoto cameras. For battery size, this smartphone is fitted with 3,046 mAh battery, which ensures that it lasts for no less than 10 hours after a complete charge.

As is present on the iPhone 11, the Pro version also rocks a dual SIM – Nano, and e-SIM. It also has the same variants in terms of storage capacity with the iPhone 11. While the 64GB goes for $999, the 256GB starts at $1,149, and the 512GB can be yours for a price tag of $1,349.

iOS 13 Environment

The iOS 13 is the newest operating system in the block released by Apple for their iPads and iPhones as well. In this update, Apple has worked on further optimizing the iOS operating system to increase its efficiency and speed as well. This optimization is present in the improvements across the iOS 13 environment.

For example, the time it took to update apps in the past has dramatically reduced, and opening and launching an app is faster than before. Downloading apps is now quicker, as download sizes have been shred down more than 50 percent. The Face ID Technology, which came in to replace the Touch ID fingerprint sensor in the iPhone XR is now faster by about 30 percent.

In addition to this, the Dark Mode debuted in this iOS 13 operating system. With the Dark Mode, users of iPhone devices running on the iOS 13 operating system can switch the entire look of their smartphone from light to dark. It allows for a custom option, and you can set Dark Mode to come on at sunset and back to light at sunrise. The Dark mode feature is present on all native apps, while third-party apps can also integrate this feature.

In addition to these other features, video editing has been made pretty possible with the use of your primary photo editing tools. Now, in the iOS 13 operating system, you will be able to carry out several edits to your videos such as cropping, rotating, adding text, or applying filters.

There are also the new Memoji and Animoji stickers that Apple has included in the iOS 13 OS. These stickers are based on your own personal Memojis and come with a lot of different expressions that you can use in messages to express emotions. They can also be used in other apps apart from Messages such as the Mail app, Contacts, etc.

iOS 13 Operating System also comes with a new app known as the Find My App. This new app is a combination of two former apps – Find My iPhone and Find My Friends app. With this app, Apple has now made it easier for users to locate all their Apple-related devices, and also find their friends close by.

One cool feature here is the ability to find a missing device whether the Wi-Fi and the cellular connection is available or not. To achieve this, Bluetooth signals given off by your Apple device can be picked up by nearby Apple devices, and you can employ that to find your missing device.

CHAPTER 2: SETTING UP YOUR DEVICE

Start and Set-up Your Device

Just as with every new device purchased, there is always the need to start and set up your device for the very first time of usage. This process helps to optimize it for usage. It also allows you to bring onboard some or most of your data from your former device to the new one. This process of starting and setting up doesn't take a lot of time but may require some crucial apps, settings, features, and the availability of internet or Wi-Fi.

Once you start your iPhone 11 for the very first time, you are greeted with the word "Hello" and a multitude of languages. Select your preferred language and then move on to selecting your country or region. This part is pretty essential as the wrong selection may mean that you'd finish the setup in an unknown language.

The next step in setting up your iPhone 11 is to select a Wi-Fi network or cellular network. If there's a Wi-Fi network in place, your iPhone will automatically detect it, and you can connect to it. You may need to use a second phone or your Mi-Fi for this purpose. Where there is none handy, simply select Cellular network.

There are two setup choices for you to flow with. The first is Automatic setup while the second is manual setup. If you were previously using an iPhone and you wish to retain the previous settings and passcodes on them, you can go with the automatic installation. The manual setup should be your choice if you are a new user. Next, click on the "Continue" button.

You can decide to enable location services now or skip it for the time being. This feature can be set up later. Thus you can click on the button that says "Enable location Services" if you wish to enable Maps and other location services. You can also click on the other button that reads "Skip Location Services" to avoid allowing location services.

The next step in setting up your new iPhone 11 is to set up your Face ID. Once you are ready to set up your Face ID, you'd see the camera frame in the middle of the screen, and you can click on the "Get Started" button to begin. You need to position your face in the middle of the frame and move your head in a circle. The aim is to ensure that all angles of your face are taken into consideration for your Face ID.

The next step would be to create a passcode for your device. For your passcode, you can either decide on the six-digit passcode or choose the four-digit passcode setup. Click on the "Passcode Options" button to change your option. With this done, you are now ready for the next phase of setting up your iPhone 11.

Restoring Data from an Old iPhone

For some users of the new iPhone devices, the question that bothers them is how they can move their data from their old iPhone to the iPhone 11. This is especially true for those who are not very technologically sound. They realize that it could be quite cumbersome to do that without someone helping out, or a guide at least. As such, there's a need to discuss this topic here.

Before now, moving and restoring your data on your new iPhone from an old one required backing it up on iCloud and restoring it while setting up the new phone. The other option was to create a backup and then restore it on your new iPhone with the help of a PC running iTunes. Any of these methods still work fine, but there are better methods now.

Now, Apple has made it possible for users to quickly move their apps and data from the old phone to the new one. This is made possible with the help of a new tool known as the iPhone migration tool. With this tool, you can either move your data via a wireless connection or a wired connection.

With the Wireless connection, you will need to start up your new phone and go through some of the processes we have discussed above. Continue with this process until you get to where you would be asked to transfer data from another phone. Accept to make the transfer and bring your old phone close to the new one.

To avoid running out of power while your data is being migrated, you may need to plug them both to a power source. On the old iPhone, you will get a pop-up message asking if you wish to set up your new iPhone. Click on the continue button, and a popup will appear on the new phone that says, "Waiting for Other iPhone." This popup also comes with an image that you will need to scan with your old iPhone.

On your old iPhone, a new notification that says, "Hold your new iPhone up to the camera" will pop up with a camera. Place your new iPhone under the camera so that it can scan the blue image. Once it scans the image successfully, you will be required to input the passcode of the old iPhone on the new one. This passcode will also be used as the passcode for the new one immediately.

The new iPhone will first be set up and then activated automatically. After this is done, you would be asked to set up the Face ID. Click on the Continue button, then Get Started. Allow the face scan to be completed as you need to do this twice. Once you are done, you would see the option to transfer your Data. This transfer can be done either directly from your old iPhone or downloading from iCloud.

The first thing to do would be to set up your Apple ID, and after that, you will need to accept the Terms and Conditions to continue. There are a few settings from your old iPhone you may need to approve the way they are or customize to fit your taste. Accept some other features or choose the option to set them up later. Once done, the transfer would begin, and you can see the notification on both iPhones.

It could take between 40 minutes to an hour for the transfer to be completed, which also depends on the amount of data you've got. You will need to ensure that both phones remain close to each other throughout the transfer. Once it is done, it shows on the old iPhone that the transfer is complete, while the new iPhone reboots and displays the Apple logo.

Once it has restarted successfully, you can now sign in to your new iPhone, and that completes the process. You will find out that apps moved to your new iPhone is dimmed. They need to be installed on your new iPhone, and that could take quite some time depending on your network.

CHAPTER 3: BASIC FUNCTIONS

How to Initiate and Answer a Call

Initiating a call via your new iPhone 11 is one of the straightforward things to do. Once you have your phone all set up and ready to use, simply locate the phone icon among the list of apps. Click on the icon, and your keypad shows up. You can now key in the number you wish to call and click on the call icon to proceed.

Alternatively, you can also go to your contacts list by clicking on the "contacts" icon below to initiate a call to a previously saved number on your contact list. If you want to return a call to a contact that earlier called you, then simply click on the "recent" button to access your "calls" list and initiate a call to any number displayed there.

Usually, to avoid missing a call, we put the ring alert tone at the highest volume. While it does its job excellently, it could also serve as a nuisance for others. Thus, if your phone is ringing and you want to shut off its sound, you can press any of the volume buttons, and the call tone is automatically muted.

Now to pick the incoming call, it's usually different depending on whether your device is locked or unlocked. Where it is locked, you'd simply need to tap on the "Slide to Answer' button and drag it to the left. However, where your smartphone is unlocked, you just need to click on the "Accept" button at the right to answer the call.

How to Divert Calls to Your Voicemail When Unavailable

There are a lot of reasons why people set voicemails, and you must learn to do so. First of all, setting up and diverting calls to your voicemail box ensures that when you are unavailable, people can drop their messages, which you can listen to later. Also, there are specific calls you may not want to pick but would wish to hear what they have to say. Voicemails make this possible.

To divert calls to your voicemails on your iPhone 11 or iPhone 11 Pro is quite easy to accomplish. Look for your phone icon and click on it. At the bottom right corner of the screen, you'd see the voicemail icon. Click on it to begin. You'd be greeted with an empty screen with the button "Set Up Now" sitting pretty in the center of your screen.

If you have previously used iPhone's voicemail service on your past iPhone, you can log in with your former password, thereby gaining access to your old voicemails. Otherwise, you will need to start the process anew. Create a new password and re-enter it. Once you are finished, click on "Done" to end the password setup.

The next step is to record a greeting. This is what the person at the other end would hear when you don't answer the phone. You can decide to use the default or create your own custom greeting sound. All you need to do is to click on "Custom" and record your personal audio. Replay it to confirm that it's okay and click on "Done" to conclude. With this, your voicemail service is set up and ready for use.

How to Check Your Voicemail

Checking your phone for voicemails you may have received while you were away is a straightforward step. First, you will need to click on the "Phone" icon. At the bottom right of your screen, you will see the voicemail button. Click on it, and you'd be presented with an empty screen with a button that says, "Call Voicemail." Click on the button and follow the instructions from your voicemail.

How to Manage Your Contacts

Managing your contacts on the iPhone 11 and 11 Pro is pretty simple and straightforward. You can easily create a new contact, delete an existing one, or change how contacts are sorted or displayed. You can also edit contacts as well, change first or last names and add other details such as email address to a contact.

All of these can be done by accessing the Contacts app in the list of the iPhone's applications. To create a new contact, follow the instructions below. You can also delete these contacts individually. To remove, select the contact you wish to delete and tap on the edit button located at the right corner of the screen. Look for the delete contact button and click on it.

Creating a New Contact

The aim of creating and storing a new contact in your address book, be it

Phone or external SIM is to ensure ease of accessibility. We are not machines, and our ability to remember is significantly limited. Thus, technology tries to help us with remembering some little things like this.

With your smartphone, you can save as many contacts as you want and simply look them up when you want to place a call across to them. You won't need to begin thinking of your partner or mum's number in your head. All you need to do is save them to your phone and access them whenever you want to. So here's how to create a new contact on iPhone 11.

In the list of apps, click on the Contacts app icon. Once in there, you'd see a "+" sign at the top right corner of your screen. That is the button for creating a new contact. Click on this button, and a form will open for the new contact you wish to create. Add the first and last names of your contact and then add the phone number.

Click on "Done" to conclude. You may also wish to add other details about your new contact. Some pieces of information you may want to add could include the company or firm where the person works, email address of your new contact, a picture, and a ringtone. All these would help in identifying who's calling at any given time.

If your new contact has more than one phone number, you can click on the "Add Phone" to add the second number. You can also do the same where there's more than one email address, as well. With this, you have successfully succeeded in creating a new contact.

How to Block Calls on iPhone 11 and iPhone 11 Pro

While the smartphone can be said to be an essential technology in our everyday life given the way it has phased out the era of letter writing, there are still some disadvantages. Previously, you could just ignore the letter in your drawer for as long as possible without giving a reply.

With the smartphone, it's no longer the same. Some people have a degree in stalking and could keep calling until your battery runs down. What to do? You only need to block their numbers on your phone, and you are safe from their constant calls and disturbances. So how do you do this?

Locate the Phone icon among your list of apps or at the bottom right corner of your phone. Tap on it, and your Keypad opens up. Look at the bottom edge and locate the "Recent" tab. There, you'd see the recent calls you have made or last incoming calls. Look for the number you wish to block and click on the "Information" icon beside the phone number or contact.

You'd see different options, but at the bottom part of the screen, there's a button that says, "Block this caller." This is where you click on to block a caller. Click on the button and on the next page that opens up, click on "Block Contact" to block or "Cancel" to leave the page without blocking the contact.

With this, you have successfully blocked the contact from calling you as calls will no longer reach you. You can rinse and repeat this process for as many numbers as you would wish to block from getting across to you

Silence Call from Unknown Number(s) on iOS 13

Unknown numbers here include calls from numbers that are not known to you or saved on your phone or hidden numbers. Sometimes, people hide their numbers to stalk others, which is also a form of cyberbullying. With your iPhone 11, you can stop calls from unknown numbers from coming in. Here's how to get that done.

Locate the Settings icon on the list of your apps and tap on it. There, you'd see some apps. Click on the one that says "Phone." Here you will see all of the settings related to calls that you can make modifications to. There's the tab that says, "Call silencing and Blocked Contacts." Below it, there's the setting that reads "Silence unknown Callers."

There's an indicator besides this setting. Click on it to turn on this feature. Once turned on, the indicator changes to green, thus indicating success. With this feature, all calls from unknown numbers are diverted to your voicemail. You can review these calls later in your free time, and if there's any you know, you can save, which would remove it from the unknown callers' list.

The Do-Not-Disturb Feature

There are basically 24 hours a day out of which we use less than 18 hours for our typical day to day activities. The remaining hours, we utilize them to sleep and rest from the day's work. Out of the 18 hours, a number of us spend a large portion fiddling with our phones that we are barely able to achieve anything.

Once there's a notification from Twitter, Instagram, Facebook, or even a message, we immediately locate our phone and spend more time than we planned on it. This has led to some people having to take drastic measures to minimize the amount of time spent on the phone. Some people put their phone on Silence mode just to cut off the notifications. Others go to the extent of putting off their phones just to avoid distractions.

While this may help in curbing the distraction, you may end up missing out on some important calls or messages. Therefore, putting off your phone or entirely placing it on silence is not the best idea for you. This is where the Do-Not-Disturb feature becomes really important.

With the Do-Not-Disturb feature, you can set your smartphone to stay in silent mode for a specific period. This period could be when you want to read, focus better, or have your siesta. No notifications are calls can come in during this period. However, you can also "whitelist" individual contacts.

These contacts are those whose calls can come in, and you get notified despite the DND feature being enabled. Say a close relative, if they call you, your phone will give you an alert despite the DND feature. To set up this feature on your iPhone 11 or iPhone 11 Pro, you need have to visit your Settings.

On the list of apps, look for the Settings icon and click on it. You'd see a host of different settings. Look for the one that says, "Do Not Disturb." Click on it, and you'd see some related settings you can edit. Close to "Do Not Disturb" at the top right of your screen, there's an indicator. Click on the symbol to turn on the DND feature.

Under this, there's the "Scheduled" option. This is where you set the DND feature to last for the number of hours you would want it to last. Enable this setting by clicking on the indicator besides this setting. It's enabled when it has a green color instead of white. Once activated, the DND feature will go off at the time you scheduled.

You can set the silent mode in DND to stay on always, or only when your iPhone is locked. Both settings are under the DND scheduling setting. If you choose the always silent mode, then your phone will never give notification alert throughout the DND period.

Where you decide to choose "While iPhone is locked," your notifications will come in, and you'd be alerted whenever your iPhone is unlocked. Once you lock it, it goes back to silent mode.

You can also set your phone to allow calls from a particular group even while on DND mode. Tap on the setting that says "Allow Calls From" and choose the group you wish to receive calls from while your iPhone is on DND. You can either choose to allow calls from families, friends, or favorites.

How to Make an Emergency Call

Making an Emergency call on your iPhone 11 is quite easy to achieve. Usually, emergency calls are made in times of trouble, crisis, or difficulties. There is, therefore, the need to be able to make such calls quickly. To ensure that emergency calls can be made speedily, Apple designed it to be fast and easy to get across to.

During an emergency, here's how to contact the emergency services without needing to key in any numbers. First of all, you need to locate and press the side button and the Volume buttons together until the slider for the emergency SOS appears on your screen.

You can drag this slider across to complete the call to Emergency services. A second option would be to continue holding down both buttons. In a few seconds, a countdown would begin, and you'd get an alert sound.

At the end of this countdown, a call will be automatically placed by your iPhone 11 to emergency services.

Once your call comes to an end, a text message is instantly sent to your Emergency Contacts. This text message contains your current location. It doesn't matter if Location Services is off, as it would temporarily come on for the message to be sent. However, you can choose to cancel sending this message.

Where your location changes, these emergency contacts will be sent an update. You'd also receive a notification 10 minutes later. Where you make use of the Emergency SOS services, you would be required to input your passcode to re-enable Touch ID. It is a strict requirement oblivious of if you completed the call or not.

The AirDrop Upgrade

The Apple AirDrop feature allows users to share pictures, documents, contacts, videos, etc. from one Apple device to another. You can use this feature to send files from an iPhone to an iPad or any of your Mac devices. This feature is quite easy to use and has recently been improved in the new iPhone 11 and iPhone 11 Pro.

The Airdrop feature was released back in 2011 on iOS 7 devices and later. This feature takes advantage of the Bluetooth and Wi-Fi technology to move files from one device to the other quickly. For it to work, AirDrop needs to be selected. This can be done by heading to the Settings app, clicking on General, and selecting AirDrop. Usually, once AirDrop has been enabled, Wi-Fi and Bluetooth are automatically enabled.

Using the AirDrop feature will require you to choose a few settings. You can either decide to allow only contacts to see your device or set it to "Everyone can see the device." The former means that only contacts stored on your phone can use this feature with you, while the latter means that anyone can see your device.

On the new iPhone range of devices, Apple has designed its U1 chip to employ the use of Ultra Wideband technology in spatial awareness. As such, the iPhone 11 can detect other Apple devices located close to it and pinpoint the one that is in a more proximal location to it.

Now, to use the AirDrop feature in sharing files to another device, all you need to do is to enable AirDrop and point your iPhone towards the other person's iPhone. Your device will automatically detect it, and you can now easily share files with them. This new feature works no matter where you are, even in a crowd with a lot of iPhone devices. The first device on your list will always be the one you point to with your own device.

Make Video Call with FaceTime

The Apple iPhone 11 series allows you to make video calls on your phone with the FaceTime App. Users of the iPhone 11 can initiate a video call to any of their contacts through several methods. Below, we shall look at some of the ways via which you can make a video call to your contacts.

- Sign in to FaceTime

To make video calls with the FaceTime app, you will need to sign in first. Tap on the FaceTime app icon to open it. You'd be required to sign in. Input your Apple ID and continue to complete the process. Your phone number is automatically registered on FaceTime if you are using an iPhone.

If you wish to add your email address to the FaceTime app, you will need to go to your settings and click on FaceTime. Input and sign in with your Apple ID, and you can now add your email address to your FaceTime.

- Making Video Calls

To make a video call with FaceTime, you will require the phone number of the contact or registered email address. The first option you have is to go through the FaceTime App. Once you open the app, click on the plus button. You will be required to input the number or email address of the contact. Input it, tap on the number and click on "video" to begin the video call. If it's a contact on your phone, start typing the name and click on it when it appears. Next, tap "video" to launch the call.

The second option is to FaceTime via your regular phone app. During a call with a contact, you can click on the

FaceTime icon that shows up. Once you do that, it would switch you automatically to a video call.

Take Screenshot on iPhone 11 and iPhone 11 Pro

Taking screenshots could be one of the most essential features ever made available on smartphones. Basically, you can use the screenshot feature to save pictures or even text that you would have ordinarily written down. For example, you're reading an article online, and you come across some important information you wish to save. Typically, you'd be inclined to write it down. However, with this feature, you can simply take a screenshot and save it to your gallery. Here's how to take a screenshot on your iPhone 11.

First of all, locate the screen or information you wish to save to your gallery. Once there, tap on the side button while also clicking on your iPhone 11's "Volume Up" button immediately. Hold steady until you hear the shutter sound and see a success notification. With this, your screenshot has successfully been saved to your gallery. You can now edit it or share it with your contacts. You can also retrieve it at any time.

CHAPTER 4: FUNCTIONALITIES SET-UP TO SUIT YOUR PERSONALITY

There are about 195 countries in the world, with over 7,000 languages spanning across different states and cities. These countries are home to over 7.7 billion people of different races, personalities, ages, and languages. There are no two same people as we are all different in one way or the other.

What you like is not what the other person will like. The language you speak may not be the same language another person speaks. While you may be American, someone else is Japanese and may not understand your language. That's why manufacturers always take these into cognizance when manufacturing goods for consumers.

Apple has also done the same in the making of their smartphones. That is why you'd find several languages on the iPhone to enable you to choose according to your personality. The same goes for the different wallpapers and fonts added here.

We shall be looking at some of the functionalities added in the iPhone 11 to ensure that users get a custom experience from each unit of iPhone they purchase.

Language Change

With over 5,000 languages across the world, it may be quite arduous to translate into all of these languages to accommodate all users. Thus, the major languages of the world need to be focused on. On the iPhone 11 and 11 Pro, you can change your language to suit your personality.

Changing your language is quite straightforward and does not require a lot of technical knowledge. To change the language on your iPhone, you need to visit the settings page via the Settings icon among the list of apps. Once you click on it, a page opens up with different settings related to the working of your phone.

Look for "General" and click on it. The 'General settings" page opens up, and you can see other settings here as well, such as Date and time, keyboard, etc. Your focus should be the Language and Region setting. Click on the Language and Region

Setting, and once it opens up, tap on the iPhone Language.

A list of all languages on the iPhone is shown here in alphabetical order, and you can now go ahead to choose your preferred language. You'd get a notification asking you to confirm if you want to change to the new language. Tap on the "Change to desired Language" or click on the Cancel button to exit the language change settings. With this, you have successfully changed your iPhone 11 or 11 Pro's language.

Use of Memojis and Animojis

The Animojis are a fun feature that debuted on the Apple iOS 11 while the Memojis were released in the succeeding version of the iOS – i.e., iOS 12. With this feature, users can create their own Animoji character, customized to look just like them. You can use the Animoji feature by going to your Messages app and starting a new message.

Next, you need to click on the icon of the little monkey. There's a plus button that you have to tap on to begin the creation of your own Animoji character. Once created, you can now go into customizing its skin tone, eyes, hair color, face shape, and a lot more.

Your Memojis can also be sent as static stickers. To do this, click on the emoji button on the keyboard. Make a choice from the available reactions and click on the three dots button to see more. You can now go ahead to choose from the ones currently available on your phone.

You can also make use of your memojis and animojis during a FaceTime call. Once you begin a FaceTime call, look towards the bottom corner and click on the little star icon. The Memojis will come up, and you can now tap on anyone you wish to use.

You can also send your selfies to friends after replacing your face with Memojis of your choice. To do this, you need to begin a new message and click on the camera icon. Once it opens, click on the star button and tap on the monkey's head icon to select the Animoji option. Once you choose your Memoji, click on the "x" button, and you can now take a selfie replacing your head with an Animoji.

Changing Wallpapers

On your iPhone 11 or 11 Pro, you can easily make changes to your wallpapers. To do this, you need to visit the settings app on your phone. Look for the Wallpaper setting and click on it. Tap the Choose a New Wallpaper and scroll through the images available. You can decide to either go with a Dynamic, Live, Still wallpapers, or a picture of yours from your gallery.

This new wallpaper can be set to serve individually as just your Home screen or Lock screen, or in both parameters. If your iPhone is locked, the wallpaper chosen for the Lock screen will show while the one selected for the Home screen appears only when your iPhone is unlocked.

You can also decide to set your wallpaper to "Still mode" so that it doesn't move when you slide through your screen, or to Perspective mode. When in Perspective, the wallpaper will move as you slide through your screen. Also, you can turn on Dark Appearance. When in this mode, your wallpaper is dimmed according to your ambient light.

Volume Control

There are two buttons on the left side of your iPhone that are used to control the volume of your media, ring tones, notifications, etc. The first is the "Volume Up" button, which allows you to increase the volume of your media. The other is the "Volume Down" button, which is used to reduce the volume of your notifications and media.

In addition to these, you can also use Siri to increase or reduce the volume of your notifications. You can simply ask Siri to "turn up the volume" or "turn down the volume," and it quickly implements it.

Adjusting the volume of your ringer alerts, sounds, and notifications can also be done from the Control Center. All you need do is to locate the Control Center, click and drag on the audio icon to increase or reduce the volume.

Accessing the Control Center

Your iPhone 11 or 11 Pro's Control Center is like a small control room that allows you to quickly access some apps and features or make changes to specific settings. Some of the things you can do from your Control Center includes toggling on or off Wi-Fi, mobile Hotspot, Bluetooth or Airplane mode settings. You can also make changes to music, access your torch, calculator, and Home screen from the Control Center.

To access the Control Center on your iPhone 11, you need to swipe down from the upper right corner of your screen. The Control Center and all the settings/features you can access on it would immediately appear. You can now make changes to whatever you would want to here.

You can also customize the Control Center to include a lot more functions or settings than it has. To personalize your Control Center, visit the Settings app. Look for Control Center and click on it. There, you can either add new settings or remove the previous ones.

Chapter 6: Top Unique Features of iPhone 11 and iPhone 11 Pro

As with all brands of phones and newer released models, consumers of these products expect that these newer models will come with unique and better features. And this is what these phone manufacturers love to do. By improving on the design and features of an earlier model, they can sell these new models at a premium price.

The iPhone 11 is not left out in this addition of unique features. All three new iPhone models were released with several essential features. These features, in turn, make the experience a beautiful one for users. We shall look at some of these newly added or upgraded features below.

Find my Phone and Find My Friend

Apple has released the new iPhone 11 with an update to some of its app. Find my Phone and Find my Friend app has been combined into one and now known as Apple Find My. With this app, you can locate your lost device, get directions to its current location, or even activate a sound notification to assist you in finding the phone. You also get to see the battery level and mark it as lost, which will enable Lost Mode to help you recover it quickly.

Another important update in the new Apple Find My app is the ability to find your device, whether it is online or offline. Therefore, even where your internet connections are all switched off, you can still locate your lost iPhone. Once another iPhone user goes past where your iPhone is, you'd get a notification with the exact location of your phone to assist you in recovering it.

To set up Find My Phone on your iPhone 11, go to your settings and click on your iPhone's name. Tap on the iCloud option and scroll all the way down to the bottom of the page. Click on Find My phone and move the slider to turn it on. Also, turn on the option to "Send Last Location." Sign in with your Apple ID if you are asked to, and all your paired devices will automatically be set up.

Extend Battery Life

While the iPhone 11 is expected to last for 11 hours, the iPhone 11 Pro goes short of about 30 minutes less than its counterpart. For what it's worth, the iPhone 11 Pro model falls short of expectations, considering its hefty prices. However, the good thing is that there are ways you can extend the battery life of your iPhone 11 to last longer than usual.

With the Low Power Mode on your phone, you can reduce the power consumption. When you enable this feature, auto-downloads, syncing of mails, and background app refreshing are disabled. You can enable this mode at any time, but usually, you'd get a notification to enable when the battery is lower than 10 percent.

Low Power Mode is enabled by going to your settings and clicking on the Battery option. There, you'd find the Low Power mode setting. Toggle it on to extend your iPhone's battery life.

The Safari Browser

On the iPhone 11 and all other iPhones, the Safari browser remains one of the most essential apps to users. With your Safari browser, you can easily access the internet and web pages on your iPhone 11. With the release of iOS 13 and the new iPhone models, several updates were made to the Safari browser to improve the browsing experience for its users.

The new Safari browser comes fitted with an updated start page, which shows your favorite websites, as well as those you frequently visit. You also get Siri suggestions from time to time on sites to visit, and links sent to you on Messages app will also pop up here.

In the newly updated Safari browser, there is a new bookmark feature that has been made available. With this feature, you can bookmark all your open tabs to be able to get to them later. All you need to do is to click and hold down the bookmark icon placed at the bottom of the Safari browser. A pop up appears, and there you can choose to "Add bookmarks for open tabs."

There's also another option that allows you to close the tabs on your Safari browser after a while. To set this up, go to Settings and click on Safari. Once there, locate the option that says "Close Tab." There, you'd see different options. Choose the one that best suits you.

With the current version of Safari, you can choose the size of your image when uploading on your iPhone 11 or 11 Pro. Simply select the picture you wish to upload and click on "Choose

Image Size" just below your Photo Library. You can now choose sizes between the Actual Size, Small, Medium, or Large.

The Face ID

The Face ID setting is one of the top new features Apple included in the latest iPhone 11 models. With the Face ID, owners of the three models of iPhone 11 can unlock their smartphones, authorize purchases on the Apple Store, or on the iTunes store. The iPhone Face ID is said to be more secure than the previous Touch ID.

Although the Face ID feature was introduced back in 2017 on the iPhone X, it has been improved on in the iPhone 11 and made more secure. What the Face ID does is to create a detailed 3D map of all parts of your face. That is why you turn your face in a circle when setting up your Face ID.

Now, whenever you want to unlock your iPhone or make a payment on the Apple Store, a secure authentication check is quickly conducted on your face. The TrueDepth Camera System, which is employed by the Face ID authentication system, detects your face with a flood illuminator no matter the time of the day, be it daylight or night.

Now, before you can use the Face ID system, you need to set it up first. Once you have successfully set up your Face ID, scans of your face will be checked with the one stored already to confirm you're the same person. This happens quite fast, and in real-time that you may never notice. Once the checks are positive, your phone is unlocked, or your payment is authorized.

So how is Face ID set up?

Setting up the Face ID authentication system on your iPhone 11 and 11 Pro is pretty simple and straight forward.

You'd need to visit your settings to get this done and over with. Look for your Settings among the list of your apps and tap on it. There's you'd see different options. Search out the one that says Face Id and Passcode. Click on it.

You'd be asked to enter your passcode. This is necessary to ensure that you are the one setting up the Face ID and not just any random person. Input your Passcode and continue. You'd see the "Enroll Face" setting under Face ID. Tap on it and click on "Get started" to continue.

You'd be shown several on-screen prompts which you are expected to follow. There's also a circular frame, and you should be able to position your face within this frame. Once you are ready to set up Face ID, click on continue and move your head slowly around. This is important to allow for a complete capture of your face.

This process of setting up your Face ID will require that two scans of your face are taken. The reason is to ensure that your face is adequately committed to the memory of the system. So even if you have to shave off your entire hair, change hairstyle, or go as far as growing a pretty huge beard, the Face ID should still be able to recognize that it's you.

Logging to Apps Using Apple ID

Ever tried to visit an app or website where you were required to sign in or sign up, and the options you had were either Google or Facebook? Well, that's what the Logging in using Apple ID brings to the table. You can now sign in to apps and websites with your Apple ID.

In iOS 13 and the current iPhone 11 models, Apple has gone ahead to release the new Sign in with Apple feature. With this sign-in feature, you can with your Apple ID, create accounts, and sign in to apps and websites. The advantage of this is that you do not have to give away any personal information, just your Apple ID.

There are not a lot of apps that allow users to enjoy the sign-in with the Apple ID feature yet, so it is currently limited. However, a deadline has been set by Google for App developers to include the feature in the apps. Therefore, before mid-2020, a lot of app developers would have added this feature to their apps.

And while Facebook and Google do virtually the same thing, Apple does it even better. On the new iPhone 11, you can employ the sign-in feature, which allows for the masking of your email, thus protecting your privacy.

How the email masking works is pretty simple.

When creating an account on an app using your Apple ID, you can decide whether to share your real email with the app or not. If you choose to share your email, the related app will receive your email address. However, if you want to mask your email, select the "Hide My Email" option.

Once you select this option, Apple generates a unique email address for you, which would be shared with the apps. Whatever correspondence there is between you and the developers or websites will go through this route.

Once these messages are delivered to you, Apple then deletes them.

You can also manage the apps and websites where you have signed in or created an account with your Apple ID on your iPhone 11. To do this, you need to visit your Settings app and tap on your profile. There, you'd need to choose the Password and Security setting. Next, you have to tap on the "Apps Using Your Apple ID" option.

A list of all apps you have signed into with your Apple ID will appear. You can now manage each one. Things you can do here include being able to see the email shared with the app if you choose the Hide My Email option. You can also choose to "Stop Using Apple ID" on that particular app. You may, however, be required to create an account when you want to use the feature again on the app.

Voice Control and Siri in iOS 13 for iPhone

The Voice Control mode in iOS 13 powered gadgets such as the iPhone 11 has been made quite all-encompassing, thereby allowing users to do a lot without having to tap or click on any buttons. With Voice Control, you can reboot your phone, make calls, navigate around your phone, play music, or open applications like Facebook or Instagram.

However, you need to set up Voice Control first before you can use it. To set up Voice Control, head over to your Settings app. look for the Accessibility option, and click on it. Once there, scroll down until you get to Voice Control. Click on it and tap on Continue. Next, click on Set up Voice Control.

Once it is set up, a blue microphone icon will appear at the top-left area of your iPhone 11 or 11 Pro and will remain while Voice Control is enabled. You can also go ahead to customize your commands and the feedback that you receive so that it is tailor suited to match your needs and interests.

You can employ the Voice Control mode to lock your iPhone, or to take screenshots. You can also say, "Turn down the volume" to reduce the volume of your sounds. When you say "Turn up the volume," the sound increases. To temporarily disable Voice Control, you can say "Go to Sleep." Re-enabling it will require you to say "Wake up" before you can use it again.

- Siri in iOS 13

Siri, on the other hand, employs Voice Control to enable you to take charge of some significant regions of your phone without the need to type. With Siri, you can request contacts saved on your Phonebook and call them, search the internet, reply to text messages, and a whole lot of other features.

Before you can make use of Siri, the internet must be active and enabled on your iPhone 11 device. Next, you have to ensure that Siri is turned on. You can press and hold the side button to get Siri activated. However, where automatic activation is enabled, you can turn Siri on by merely saying, "Hey Siri."

Whatever you want your device to do for you, simply say it, and Siri will respond with the feature. You can make calls, open your camera, and search the internet. To personalize your experience, you can also add shortcuts to Siri to help you fast track your requests.

On iOS 13, several improvements to Siri has been made. Now, when you send messages with Siri, a notification appears underneath your message that it was sent using Siri. Thus, you may not be blamed for some of the errors

Siri makes when you reply to messages.

In the Maps application, Siri has been made better and more specific. Directions such as "… in 500 feet, turn left" have been eliminated. Instead, Siri would say something like, "Turn right at the next street." As such, your directions have been made more explicit as you quickly know when to turn left or stop at a traffic light.

The Haptic Touch

The Haptic Touch setup is yet another one of Apple's unique Technology for the iPhone 11 models of phones. Although it featured in the iPhone XR released back in 2018, it has been made a whole lot better with the latest iPhone 11 releases. The Haptic Touch technology replaces the 3D Touch technology previously employed by Apple.

And while the 3D Touch technology was built to rely on pressure to perform, Haptic Touch is a shift away from that system. Instead, for Haptic Touch to work, it requires the user to long press on the screen. A small vibration soon follows, and if a shortcut is available, it will appear.

With Haptic Touch, you get to do things faster than when it was the 3D Touch Technology. For example, you want to take a picture on your phone. Haptic Touch allows you to take your picture without even having to open your camera app. Simply long-press on the camera icon and select from the list of options that appear.

The Haptic Touch Technology works with almost all the native apps present on the iPhone 11 and even some third-party apps as well. If you want to share your location or view a place nearby, you don't need to open your Maps application. Simply long-press on the Maps icon and select what you want to do from the shortcut that appears.

The same goes for your clock. Without actually opening the clock app, you can set, create a new alarm or set a stopwatch to begin running. In the case of the Phone app, the Haptic Touch technology will allow you to create a new contact, search for an already existing contact or even view your recent calls.

To allow for a better experience with the Haptic Touch, Apple will enable customers to change the sensitivity options for this technology. There are two options you can choose from – either fast or slow. If you select "Fast," you will only need to press on an icon for a short while before the shortcut menu appears. Slow will do the opposite.

To change the sensitivity of the Haptic Touch, you would need to visit the Settings app and head over to Accessibility. Look for the Touch setting and click on it. You'd see Haptic Touch. Click on it and select any of the two sensitivity options, i.e., fast or slow. To simply put it, the Haptic Touch Technology was brought in to replace the 3D Touch technology to ease operation time and that it has done so far.

Gestures and Buttons

For a significant part of previous iPhone releases, Apple made sure to always include a home button until recently. In fact, the reign of the Home button on iPhones was ended in the version of the iPhone X. It, therefore, wasn't shocking when the iPhone 11 models were released, and it was all edge to edge display, no Home buttons.

While it could be a hard pill to swallow for those who had come to get so used to the Home button, Apple made it pretty easy for users to return to their Home Screen effortlessly. To do this, the user would simply need to swipe upwards from the bottom of the screen.

There are some other buttons on the iPhone 11, such as the two volume buttons on the left side of the phone and a side button on the right side. There is also a ring/silent selector above the volume buttons on the left side. The primary use of the volume buttons is to increase and decrease the volume of your sounds.

With the ring/silent selector, you can disable ring out on your iPhone or enable it. When disabled, no ringtones and notification tones are played when calls or messages come in. If you enable it, then the opposite happens. The Side button is used to turn on or wake your iPhone 11 or 11

Pro. Using it in combination with other buttons can do a lot more.

For example, you need to press both the Side button and any of the volume buttons to bring up the Shutdown screen. Next, slide on the screen to turn off your iPhone 11. If you want to bring up Apple Pay, you would need to double press the Side button. To take a screenshot, you can use the Side button plus the Volume Up button.

You can also temporarily disable Face ID on your iPhone 11 using a combination of buttons. With your iPhone screen off, you'd need to press and hold down on the Side button in addition to any Volume button. Face ID would be temporarily disabled until the next time you lock your screen.

If you want to use Siri on your phone, you'd need to press and hold down the Side button until Siri comes up. If you wish to bring up SOS on your iPhone 11, your best bet would be to press and hold the side button while combining it with any of the volume buttons. SOS comes up, and you can do your thing.

With the removal of the Home button on the iPhone, several gestures were introduced. It's now straightforward switching between apps on the iPhone

11 and 11 Pro. To switch between apps, you have to touch the gesture area at the bottom of your iPhone 11 display and swipe from left to right to return to the previous app. For the next app, you'd need to swipe from right to left.

On your iPhone 11 or 11 Pro, bringing up the multitasking fast app switcher requires the use of a gesture. You'd need to place your finger at the bottom of your iPhone 11 screen display, which is where the gesture area is located. Slightly swipe your finger in an upward manner, and the multitasking app switcher opens. You can now easily switch between several open apps.

With the gesture feature, you can also force quit or kill the running apps in the system. You need to first bring up the multitasking fast app switcher by placing your finger on the gesture area and swiping up slightly. Once it opens, you can then swipe up on any of the open app cards to force quit the app. With this, you can kill as many apps as you want.

You can also access your widgets using the gesture feature. Simply swipe right from your home screen, and your Widgets would pop up immediately. If you have previously added apps to the widget, you can find information about them here. You can also use the edit button at the bottom of the widgets to edit what you want to be displayed on your widgets.

If you want to do a search for something on your phone or on the internet, you can achieve this quickly by swiping down from the middle of the screen. There' you will see the search input bar. Type in what you are looking for and click on the search button.

You can also access the Control Center on your iPhone 11 or 11 Pro. The Control Center allows you to quickly make changes to settings on your smartphone or use some apps. From the upper-right corner of your screen, swipe down, and there you have it – your Control Center.

You can also easily view apps, phone calls, SMS, reminders, and alarm notifications on your phone with the gesture feature. By swiping downwards from the top of your screen, you can see these notifications. There are some other gestures, but these are the basic ones you'd need to get through every day on your new iPhone 11.

Dark Mode on iPhone 11

If you use an iPhone 11 or 11 Pro, then welcome to the world of everything dark. On your iPhone, you can easily switch your phone from light to Dark mode and back. This is a useful upgrade as it helps to improve readability, and its importance is better noticed in dimly lighted environments. Unlike when it was limited to stand-alone apps, Dark mode is system-wide on iOS 13 devices such as the iPhone 11 and 11 Pro.

It's quite easy to enable Dark Mode on your iPhone device. Visit your Settings page and click on the Display

& Brightness option. Quickly choose the Dark option, and it is immediately implemented system-wide on your phone. You can also set it on Automatic so that it switches between light and dark mode automatically.

CONCLUSION

The iPhone 11 and 11 Pro are just two out of the three major releases by Apple this year. And they are also the cheapest, although they aren't so pocket friendly. However, Apple went a whole distance in making them the kind of gadgets everyone would want to be seen with.

On the iPhone 11 models, Apple had a focus on delivering superior and edge cutting technology to their cameras. This has so far seen the introduction of a three camera system, and night mode to take better shots at night, as well as low-light environments. Videos are also not left out here as you can now easily take and edit your videos from your iPhone.

A lot of the basic functions, and the new amazing features that have been made available in the iPhone 11 and 11 Pro have been discussed at length in this book. The Airdrop feature, the improved Face ID, and even how to make a FaceTime video are discussed here. So go ahead and have fun with your new smartphone, while using this "guide as a guide".